Piranhas

by Emily McAuliffe

Content Consultant:
Dr. Leo Nico
U.S. Department of the Interior
Florida Caribbean Science Center

RiverFront Books

An Imprint of Franklin Watts
A Division of Grolier Publishing
New York   London   Hong Kong   Sydney
Danbury, Connecticut

RiverFront Books
http://publishing.grolier.com
Copyright © 1998 by Capstone Press. All rights reserved.
Published simultaneously in Canada.

Printed in the United States of America.

Library of Congress Cataloging-in-Publication Data
McAuliffe, Emily.
    Piranhas /by Emily McAuliffe.
    p. cm.--(Dangerous animals)
    Includes bibliographical references and index.
    Summary: Details the physical characteristics, behavior, natural habitat,
and life cycle of this commonly-feared fish found in South American rivers.
    ISBN 1-56065-620-4
    1. Piranhas--Juvenile literature. [1. Piranhas. 2. Fishes.]
I. Title. II. Series.
QL638.C5M335   1998
597'.48--dc21

                                                97-8317
                                                  CIP
                                                   AC

Photo credits
Heather Angel, 34
FPG/Toby Molenaar, 10
John Shedd Aquarium, 12, 39; Patrice Ceisel, 16, 22, 42
Natural History Photography/André Bärtschi, 24, 28
Nature's Images/David Schleger, 6, 18, 26, 31, 32
Unicorn Stock/Chris Boylan, 14; Doris Brookes, 41
Brian Vikander, 8, 36
Visuals Unlimited/Kjell Sandved, cover, 21

Table of Contents

Fast Facts about Piranhas

Scientific Name: Piranhas are grouped into the family Characidae. Piranhas are put into either the *Serrasalmus, Pygocentrus, Pristobrycon,* or *Pygopristis* genera. A genus is a group of closely related plants or animals. There are at least 30 different species of piranhas. A species is a group of similar animals that can mate with each other.

Size: Different kinds of piranhas are different sizes. Most kinds are 10 to 14 inches (25 to 36 centimeters) long. The San Francisco piranha or piraya is one of the largest species of piranha. It grows to at least 20 inches (51 centimeters) long.

Coloring: Coloring depends on the kind of piranha. The white or spotted piranha is light colored when it is young. When it is older, it turns dark gray or olive-colored. There are large, dark spots scattered on its back and sides. The

4

tail fin is reddish with dark edges. A young red piranha has a bright red throat, stomach, and fins.

Habitat: Piranhas live in rivers, lakes, and lagoons. A lagoon is a shallow pool of water surrounded by land.

Range: Piranhas are only found in South America. Many piranhas live in the Amazon which is the second longest river in the world.

Food: Piranhas eat many things. Most people think piranhas feed only on meat. But many scientists have also found seeds and fruits in piranhas' stomachs.

Behavior: Piranhas often live and travel in groups that are called schools. Schools are usually small. But in some cases they can contain up to 300 fish.

Chapter One

The Piranha

There are many species of piranhas. A species is a group of similar animals that can mate with each other. Only four piranha species are believed to be dangerous to humans. The rivers of South America are the only places flesh-eating piranhas are found in the wild. Even so, piranhas are among the most feared fish in the world.

Most piranhas are not very large. But their strong jaws are filled with razor-sharp teeth. These teeth tear chunks of flesh out of a victim.

Piranhas sometimes travel alone. They also travel in groups that are called schools. Piranha schools usually include less than 36 fish swimming and hunting together. Schools of fish also eat together. A piranha school can

Piranhas are among the most feared fish in the world.

Many kinds of piranhas live in the Amazon.

turn a large animal into a skeleton. In seconds, piranhas can eat all the animal's flesh and muscle.

Eating can be dangerous for piranhas. Hungry piranhas may accidentally take bites out of each other. They do this as they are trying to attack and eat their food.

Ichthyology
The Greek word for fish is ichthys. This is why the study of fish is called ichthyology.

Piranhas are vertebrates. Vertebrates are animals with backbones inside their bodies. The largest group of fish is known as the bony fish. Piranhas are part of this group.

Range

Piranhas are cold-blooded. This means that they receive body heat from their surroundings. Warm water is best for piranhas. Piranhas would die if they were in cold water. This is why piranhas live mostly in warm areas of South America. Colombia, Venezuela, the Guianas, Peru, Ecuador, Uruguay, Bolivia, Brazil, and Paraguay have piranhas in their rivers.

Most people think of the Amazon when they think of piranhas. Many kinds of piranha live in this river. The Amazon is the second longest river in the world. It flows more than 4,087 miles (6,539 kilometers) from the Andes mountains in Peru into the Atlantic Ocean.

The land this river flows through is called the Amazon basin or Amazonia. More than 24 Amazonian towns and land features are named after piranhas. Scientists studying a single river

Piranha teeth can clip a mouthful of flesh from prey.

in Amazonia found six different species of piranha living in it.

Teeth and Jaws

Piranha teeth are not designed to crush or hold prey. Prey are animals that are hunted and eaten for food. Instead, piranha teeth are made to clip a mouthful of flesh from prey. This turns the prey into small pieces the piranha can swallow. A piranha takes many bites every minute. Their teeth also help them bite parts of hard seeds.

An average piranha bite removes a cherry-sized chunk of flesh. Bites are this small because a piranha's mouth is small. Its jaws are short and wide. Powerful muscles open and close both the lower and upper jaws. The lower jaw is especially powerful.

Each jaw contains a single row of triangle-shaped teeth. This makes the row of teeth like a saw blade. A piranha's teeth are similar in sharpness to a shark's teeth. The teeth of the upper jaw glide against the teeth of the lower jaw. This helps a piranha's teeth easily slice through its food.

Indians who live in Amazonia have many uses for piranha teeth. Some people use the teeth to cut things. Sometimes the tooth-filled jaws are used like scissors. Amazonian hunters use the teeth to make arrowheads.

Body and Fins

Piranhas are flat, oval-shaped fish. Their flat body shape helps them swim quickly through the water.

Most fish have fins. Fins help fish stop or move in almost any direction. They also help fish keep their balance while they are swimming. Piranhas have five kinds of fins that help them swim.

One kind of fin is the tail fin. Scientists call this the caudal fin. The second kind of fin is a dorsal fin. This is the large fin near the middle of a piranha's back.

The third kind of fin is an anal fin. This single fin is on a piranha's lower side near the caudal fin. Piranhas also have a pair of pectoral fins and a pair of ventral fins. Pectoral fins are on a piranha's sides. These fins help piranhas change directions while they are swimming.

Scales

Like most fish, piranhas are covered with scales. Their scales overlap and protect their bodies.

Piranhas are flat, oval-shaped fish.

Piranhas' scales grow larger as they grow.

Scales are really an extension of a fish skin. They are colorless. Piranhas receive their color from body parts under the scales.

Piranhas have glands in their skin. A gland is a body organ that produces natural chemicals. The glands in piranhas' skin produce a slime layer. This protects piranhas from disease and helps them move quickly through the water.

A slime layer protects piranhas from disease.

Chapter Two

Survival

All creatures need oxygen to survive. Piranhas are no different. Yet piranhas and other fish do not have lungs like humans and other land animals. Instead, they have a gill system. A gill is an organ on a fish's side that helps it breathe.

To breathe, piranhas take water into their mouths. Then they force the water back out of their mouths and over their gills. The surface of the gills is very thin. The gills take oxygen from the water. The oxygen then travels into piranhas' bloodstream. This process gives piranhas the oxygen they need to live.

Food
Piranhas are predators. A predator is an animal that survives by hunting other animals for food.

Piranhas have a gill system that helps them breathe.

Some kinds of piranhas eat the fins of other fishes.

Piranhas usually eat small fish. They also eat dead or wounded animals.

Some piranha species eat the scales off other fish. This is called lepidophagy. Many young piranhas bite and eat the fins of other fish. Most of these fins and scales grow back.

Piranhas are best-known for being deadly, meat-eating fish. But many piranhas are omnivores. An omnivore is an animal that eats both flesh and plants. Piranhas feed on seeds and fruits when meat is not available. Some piranhas seem to prefer eating seeds even when meat is available.

Rainy Season
The rainy season is very important to piranhas. The rainy season is a period of time with increased rainfall in the Amazon. The rivers flood. The water covers the surface of the surrounding forest.

The flooded forest is an important source of food for piranhas. They swim into the forest. There they eat fruits, seeds, and grains not available during the rest of the year.

As the waters return to normal levels, most piranhas return to the river. But some piranhas become trapped in lagoons. A lagoon is a shallow pool of water surrounded by land. The Sun often dries out lagoons. Any piranhas left in the lagoon die without the water. Even if the lagoons do not dry up, piranhas often run out of food. They starve if the rainy season does not return soon enough. Starve means to suffer or die from lack of food.

Senses

Like humans, piranhas have well-developed senses. Piranhas can see, hear, smell, feel, and taste. All these senses are important when piranhas search for food.

Piranhas are also able to sense water vibrations. This helps piranhas find and catch their prey. When objects fall or travel through water, they send out vibrations. These vibrations travel well through water.

Piranhas' bodies are built to sense these vibrations. They have small hairs that grow in pores on their sides. The hair and pores together are called the lateral line. The hairs detect motion in the water around piranhas. This alerts them to the presence of an enemy, possible prey, or falling seeds and fruits.

Piranhas are attracted by movements in the water. A struggling animal or fish sends vibrations through the water. Schools of piranha then race toward the struggling or injured creature. Each piranha uses its razor-

Schools of piranha will attack struggling victims.

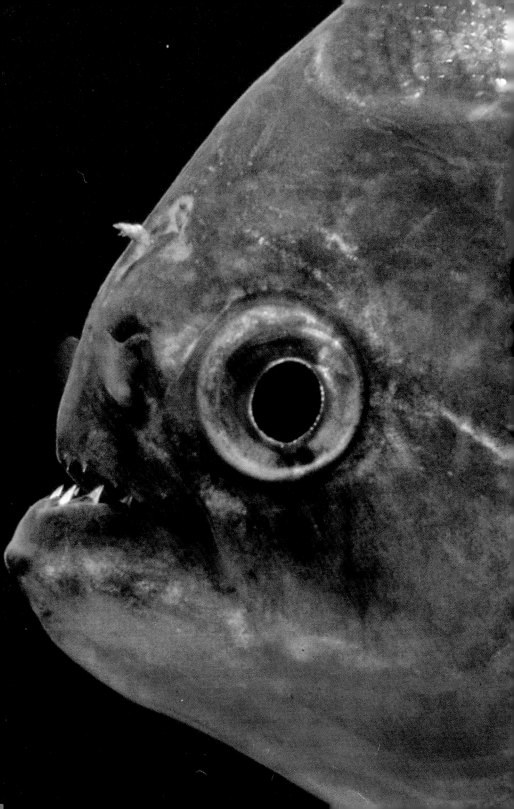

sharp teeth to bite a chunk of the victim's flesh. Piranha attacks are violent and quick. The water around them fills with blood. The blood makes the piranhas more excited. Their bodies move back and forth so quickly that the water becomes disturbed.

Blood

Some scientists believe piranhas have a strong sense of smell. Like humans, piranhas have nostrils that they use to smell. Piranhas have four nostrils. Water flows into the nostrils and into a small sac just below the skin. The sacs have special cells that sense odor in the water.

Scientists believe that piranhas can smell blood in the water. This would make piranhas like sharks. Sharks can smell blood from up to one-quarter mile (about one-half kilometer) away. Blood in water probably attracts piranhas.

Piranhas use their four nostrils to smell blood.

Chapter Three

A Piranha's Life

Little is known about how piranhas mate and reproduce in the wild. Piranhas are difficult to study while alive. Scientists believe that female piranhas spawn during the start of the rainy season. Spawn means to lay eggs.

Spawning

Scientists do not know exactly where piranhas spawn. They do know that some piranhas make shallow nests.

Sometimes piranhas snip off plants to make a hollow for their nests. Females lay hundreds of eggs in the nests.

Piranhas are difficult to study while they are alive.

Newly hatched piranhas are called fry.

Fry

After four days, the eggs hatch. Newly hatched piranhas are called fry. The newborn fry are blind. They eat the yolk that is left in their eggs.

26

After six days, their eyes develop enough for them to see.

The parents guard fry. This helps keep fry safe from other predators. As they grow older, young piranhas may eat seeds and fruits in the flooded forest where they hatched.

Growth

Soon after birth, fry begin to develop scales. Their teeth begin to appear. They grow larger. If piranhas have enough food, they will continue to grow throughout their lives. Some kinds of piranhas grow at least 20 inches (51 centimeters) long.

Piranhas grow the fastest during the first few years of life. They grow more slowly as they grow older.

Chapter Four

Common Kinds of Piranha

There are many species of piranha. At least 25 different species of fish are called piranhas.

Redeye Piranha

The redeye piranha is also known as the piranha preta in Amazonia. An adult's color ranges from dark blue to dark black. All adults have red eyes. A young redeye is silver and spotted. Its fins are clear like glass.

The redeye piranha is one of the most common kinds of piranha in the Amazon. This species of piranha is considered dangerous to humans. An adult's jaws are so strong that they

The redeye piranha is known for its red eyes.

can snap off a man's hand at the wrist in only three bites. Redeye piranhas frequently hunt and attack prey.

Redeye piranhas are also one of the larger kinds of piranha. Adults can grow to 18 inches (46 centimeters) long. They weigh up to four and one-half pounds (two kilograms).

Redeye piranhas mostly dine on fish that they catch during the day. During the rainy season, they feast on seeds and fruits. Redeye piranhas have also been known to attack birds, water lizards, and small animals. Sometimes they eat beetles and crabs.

Redeye piranhas hunt during the day. Occasionally they hunt at night. They hide in plant life found on the sides and bottoms of rivers. They rush out of hiding and attack their prey from behind. They usually will not swim after prey if their first attack does not succeed. Because they attack from behind, scientists find many fish tails in piranhas' stomachs.

It is rare that one redeye piranha has a chance to eat a whole fish by itself. This is

The slender piranha has a long head and snout.

because piranhas hunt in small schools. All the piranhas in a school will eat the prey. Each piranha eats some mouthfuls of the prey's flesh.

Slender Piranha

The slender piranha is also known as the opossum piranha. In Amazonia, it is known as piranha mucura. It has a longer head and snout. A snout is the long, front part of an animal's head. The nose, mouth, and jaws are part of the snout.

Slender piranha grow to about 11 inches (28 centimeters) long. They are not considered as harmful to humans. But they do hunt prey.

The slender piranha mostly eats the fins and scales of other fish. They attack their prey from behind and sometimes from the side. Slender piranha usually attack the caudal fin. Sometimes they go after the anal fin.

Usually, fish survive these attacks. They grow new scales and fins. But some fish show scars. These fish's caudal and anal fins have missing chunks from the attack.

Red Piranha

The red piranha is one of the most common species of piranha in Amazonia. It is easy to spot because of its coloring. A young red piranha has a bright red throat, stomach, and fins. This color fades as it grows older. Adult coloring ranges from brownish to blue-gray. Adults grow to 13 inches (30 centimeters) long. Their coloring makes red piranhas popular aquarium fish.

The red piranha is a popular aquarium fish.

Red piranhas are known as one of the fiercest piranha species. They hunt and eat prey. But like redeye piranha, they eat fruits and seeds during the flood season.

Filmmakers also used red piranhas in movies. They cut off piranhas' lips so their sharp teeth would show. They made it look like schools of piranha would attack any person who went in the water. The movies were wrong about piranhas. The movies made red piranhas seem more dangerous than they are.

Chapter Five

Piranha and People

Hundreds of years ago, European explorers returned from the Amazon with stories about piranha. They called them devil fish. President Theodore Roosevelt was one Amazonian explorer. He said that piranha were evil.

Because of these stories, people became afraid of piranha. But piranha serve a purpose. They eat dead and wounded animals that fall into rivers. They also eat sick fish. This keeps the rivers clean from rotting flesh.

Piranhas rarely attack healthy fish or animals. They usually hunt things that are weak, hurt, or sick. Piranhas can eat sick fish and animals without becoming sick themselves.

Piranhas rarely attack healthy fish or animals.

Many people who fish attach thick wire to their fishing lines.

By eating sick animals, piranhas are helping the Amazon and other rivers stay healthy.

Piranha and Amazonians
People who live in Amazonia know that piranhas are important to the Amazon. They have learned to live with piranha. People can swim in piranha-filled water without being attacked. But they must know when to avoid piranha-filled water.

Amazonians follow safety measures when dealing with piranhas.

People avoid lagoons that hold trapped piranhas. They know the piranhas there are starving and will attack almost anything that falls into the water. People also do not swim in water that contains blood. They know blood excites piranhas and makes them attack.

Piranhas are an important food source for Amazonians. They eat piranha head soup.

Piranhas and Fishing

Piranhas can be a problem to people who fish in Amazonia. Piranhas that are hooked or netted twist fiercely and snap their powerful jaws. It is easy to get bitten by captured piranhas. People must make sure piranhas are dead before bringing them into the boat.

Piranhas can easily bite through normal fishing lines. Many people attach thick wire to their fishing lines. This makes it harder for piranha to bite through the lines.

Some people use nets to catch fish. Piranhas often attack fish that are caught in the nets.

When this happens, piranhas also wreck the nets. Some nets can be fixed, but many nets are damaged beyond repair. Replacing nets due to piranha attacks becomes a big expense.

Piranhas and Cattle

Many people in the Amazon make a living by herding cattle. Piranhas can be dangerous to cattle, too. But real attacks on cattle are rare.

Some piranhas bite cattle's noses when they try to drink water. Although the bites are not deadly, the wounds could make cattle sick. Sometimes piranhas attack cattle when they are crossing a river. Usually cattle walk through water undisturbed.

Piranhas do not normally attack large, healthy animals. In fact, piranhas tend to swim away from South American alligators called caiman. Piranhas also will often swim away from people that dive with masks on.

Aquarium Fish

People outside of Amazonia also became interested in piranhas. In the 1970s and 1980s,

Piranhas once were popular aquarium fish.

piranhas became a popular aquarium fish. Piranha owners fed their piranhas smaller fish or pieces of meat.

State officials feared that someone might release piranhas into local waters. Then piranhas might live and breed. New laws were made to stop this from happening.

Today, owning a piranha is illegal in many states. People who ship piranhas to the United States must have special permits.

Piranha Attacks
Most tales of piranha attacks on humans are greatly exaggerated. Exaggerate means to make something seem bigger and more important than it is. Whether the tales are true or not, all piranhas must be treated carefully. People cannot safely guess how wild animals will act.

At some river crossings in South America, guards warn travelers. They tell travelers that piranhas live in the water. Once people know that piranhas are present, they will cross the river carefully. People with scrapes or wounds will not be safe in the water. Blood might attract the piranhas.

Future
Many areas of the Amazon rain forest are being cut down and developed. This disturbs piranhas' living areas. When the river floods, there is not as much forest left. It becomes harder for piranhas to find the seeds, fruits, and grains they eat.

People are trying to clear rivers of piranha.

People affect piranhas in other ways. In some places, people are trying to clear rivers of all piranha. People have put other large fish like peacock cichlids in rivers in the hopes of cutting down piranha populations. Peacock cichlids attack and eat young piranha.

As more rain forest is destroyed, the future of piranhas becomes more uncertain. Piranhas are needed to help keep the Amazon healthy.

Scales

Gills

Nostrils

Powerful
Lower Jaw

Pectoral
Fin

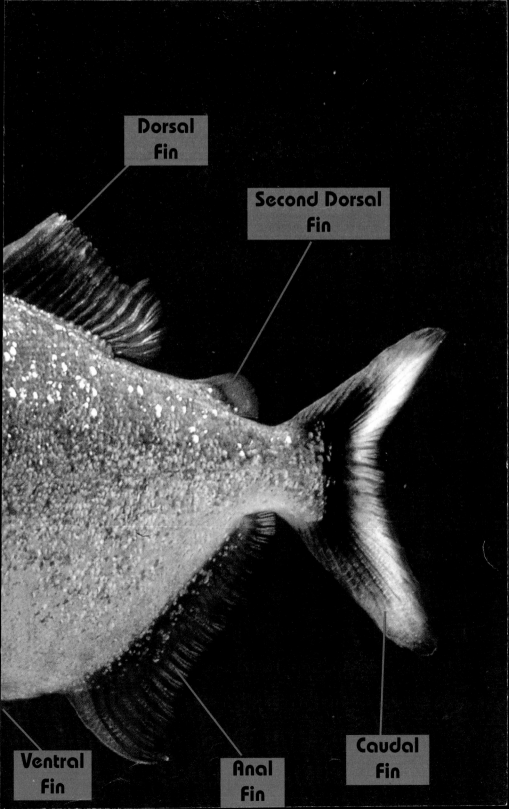

Dorsal
Fin

Second Dorsal
Fin

Ventral
Fin

Anal
Fin

Caudal
Fin

Words to Know

gill (GIL)—an organ fish use to get oxygen out of water

ichthyology (ik-thee-AHL-oh-gee)—the scientific study of fish and fish behavior

lepidophagy (le-pid-AHF-ah-gee)—the process of eating another fish's scales

omnivore (OM-nuh-vor)—an animal that eats both flesh and plants

predator (PRED-uh-tur)—an animal that lives by hunting and eating other animals

scale (SKALE)—one of many small, thin plates that cover a fish's body

school (SKOOL)—a large number of the same kind of fish swimming and feeding together

spawn (SPAWN)—to produce eggs

vertebrate (VUR-tuh-brit)—an animal that has a backbone

To Learn More

Broekel, Ray. *Dangerous Fish*. Chicago: Children's Press, 1982.

Freedman, Russell. *Killer Fish*. New York: Holiday House, 1982.

Grossman, Susan M. *Piranhas*. New York: Dillon Press, 1994.

Lenga, Rosalind. *The Amazing Fact Book of Fish*. Mankato, Minn.: Creative Education, 1988.

Schleser, David M. *Piranhas: Everything About Origins, Care, Feeding, Diseases, Breeding, and Behavior*. Hauppauge, N.Y.: Barrons Educational Series, 1997.

Useful Addresses

Aquatic Conservation Network
540 Roosevelt Avenue
Ottawa, Ontario K2A 1Z8
Canada

National Marine Fisheries Service
7600 Sand Point Way NE
Seattle, WA 98115

U.S. Fish and Wildlife Services
1849 C Street NW
Washington, DC 20240

World Aquaculture Society
143 J.M. Parker Coliseum
Louisiana State University
Baton Rouge, LA 70803

Internet Sites

An Amazon Adventure—Animals
http://ogms.hanc.k12.wv.us/amazon/animal.htm

Electronic Zoo
http://netvet.wustl.edu/e-zoo.htm

Floater PiranhaCam
http://www.ultranet.com/~floater/pirancam.htm

Piranha
http://rif27.iac.org.nz/Animals/piranha.htm

ZooNet
http://www.mindspring.com/~zoonet

Index

Amazon, 5, 9, 19, 29, 36, 38, 40, 41

Amazonia, 9, 10, 11, 29, 31, 33, 35, 36, 37, 39

anal fin, 13, 33

blood, 23, 37

cattle, 38

caudal fin, 13, 33

dorsal fin, 13

eggs, 25, 27

food, 5, 8, 11, 17, 19, 20, 27, 37

fry, 27

gill, 17

gland, 15

ichthyology, 8

jaws, 11, 37

nostril, 23

omnivore, 18

pectoral fin, 13

predator, 17

prey, 10, 11, 20, 29, 30, 33

rainy season, 19, 25, 30, 33

red piranha, 5, 33

redeye piranha, 29-30, 33

Roosevelt, Theodore, 35

scale, 13, 15, 18, 27, 32

school, 5, 7, 8, 30

slender piranha, 31-32

snout, 31

spawn, 25

tail fin, 13

teeth, 7, 10, 11, 23, 37

ventral fin, 13